Pebble®
Plus

GREAT ASIAN AMERICANS

Ellison Onizuka

by Stephanie Cham

CAPSTONE PRESS
a capstone imprint

Pebble Plus is published by Capstone Press,
1710 Roe Crest Drive, North Mankato, Minnesota 56003
www.mycapstone.com

Cataloging-in-Publication Data is available on the Library of Congress website
ISBN: 978-1-5157-9956-6 (library binding)
ISBN: 978-1-5157-9971-9 (paperback)
ISBN: 978-1-5157-9977-1 (eBook PDF)

Editorial Credits
Abby Colich, editor; Juliette Peters, designer;
Morgan Walters, media researcher; Kathy McColley, production specialist

Photo Credits
ASSOCIATED PRESS: NASA, 5; Getty Images: Historical, 17; Newscom: NASA/UPI, Cover, 15,
SISSON/SIPA, 19; Shutterstock: Angel DiBilio, 11, Attitude, design element throughout,, Eugene
Berman, 9, Ingus Kruklitis, 13, j avarman, (pattern) design element throughout, KYPhua, 7, most
popular, design element throughout, Supannee_Hickman, 21

Note to Parents and Teachers

The Great Asian Americans set supports standards related to biographies.
This book describes and illustrates the life of Ellison Onizuka. The images
support early readers in understanding the text. The repetition of words
and phrases helps early readers learn new words. This book also introduces
early readers to subject-specific vocabulary words, which are defined in the
Glossary section. Early readers may need assistance to read some words and
to use the Table of Contents, Glossary, Read More, Internet Sites, Critical
Thinking Questions, and Index sections of the book.

Printed and bound in the USA.
010771S18

Table of Contents

Early Life 4

Early Work 8

Working at NASA 12

Glossary 22

Read More 23

Internet Sites 23

Critical Thinking Questions 24

Index 24

Early Life

Ellison Onizuka was born in 1946.
He lived in Hawaii. Ellison had
two sisters and one brother.
He played sports. He was
a boy scout.

1946
born June 24
in Hawaii

Ellison went to college in 1964.

He studied to be an engineer.

He was in ROTC. ROTC gets

students ready for the military.

1964
begins at the University
of Colorado, Boulder

1969
receives bachelor's
and master's degrees

1946

Early Work

After college Ellison joined
the Air Force. He was
a pilot. He tested planes.
He helped make them safer.

1970
joins U.S. Air Force

1946   1964   1969

Ellison went to a school
for Air Force pilots in 1974.
He learned how to test
new planes. Then he worked
at the school.

1974
begins U.S. Air Force
Test Pilot School

1975
begins working at
Edwards Air Force
Base in California

1946   1964   1969   1970

Working at NASA

Ellison was in the Air Force for eight years. Then he wanted to be an astronaut. He went to work at NASA. He trained for one year.

1978
begins working at NASA

1979
finishes training

For the eyes of the world now look into space,
to the moon and to the planets beyond,
and we have vowed that we shall not see
it governed by a hostile flag of conquest,
but by a banner of freedom and peace.
— John F. Kennedy

Ellison did many jobs at NASA.

He helped shuttles take off.

He worked on test flights.

Astronauts trained on the flights.

They felt like they were in space.

Ellison went to space in 1985.

He flew on the *Discovery*.

It flew around Earth

for 74 hours. The crew

did work for the military.

1985
goes into space
for the first time

The next year Ellison

was ready to go back to space.

He got on the *Challenger.*

It took off. Then it broke apart.

Everyone inside died.

1986
dies on the
Challenger

1946   1964   1969   1970   1974   1975   1978   1979   1985

19

Ellison was buried

in his hometown.

He was the first

Asian-American astronaut.

He is still remembered today.

2017
the 17th Astronaut
Onizuka Science
Day is celebrated

1946   1964   1969   1970   1974   1975   1978   1979   1985   1986

monument to
Ellison Onizuka
in Los Angeles

21

Glossary

Air Force—the part of the U.S. military that's trained to fight with aircraft

crew—a team of people who work together

engineer—a person who uses science and math to plan, design, or build

military—the armed forces of a state or country

NASA—a U.S. government agency that does research on flight and space exploration; NASA stands for National Aeronautics and Space Administration

ROTC—a program that teaches its members military leadership skills while they attend college; ROTC stands for Reserve Officers' Training Corps

shuttle—a spacecraft that takes astronauts into space and back to Earth

Read More

Clay, Kathryn. *Astronaut in Training.* Little Astronauts. North Mankato, Minn.: Capstone, 2017.

Rustad, Martha E. H. *Working in Space.* An Astronaut's Life. North Mankato, Minn.: Capstone, 2018.

Stone, Adam. *The Challenger Explosion.* Disaster Stories. Minneapolis, Minn.: Bellwether Media, 2014.

Internet Sites

Use FactHound to find Internet Sites related to this book.

Visit *www.facthound.com*

Just type in 9781515799566 and go.

Check out projects, games and lots more at
www.capstonekids.com

Critical Thinking Questions

1. Reread page 6. What is ROTC?
2. What is one way astronauts train before going into space?
3. What was the name of the space shuttle Ellison flew on in 1985?

Index

Air Force, 8, 10, 12
astronauts, 14, 20

childhood, 4
college, 6, 8

death, 18

Earth, 16

Hawaii, 4

military, 6, 16

NASA, 12, 14

planes, 8, 10

ROTC, 6

shuttles, 14, 16, 18
space, 14, 16, 18

training, 12